Franck Choquet

Wonderful Côtes-du-Nord

Translated by Angela Moyon

Front cover : *Ploumanac'h.*

Back cover : *Dinan.*

Top to bottom :
In the Plestin area.
Fort-La-Latte.
The harbour at Binic.

The "Celtic Sea" - view from Cap Fréhel.

This is a *département* with four faces. On the Channel coast is the Armor (the country of the sea); inland is the Argoat (the country of woods). To the west lies the Breton-speaking Lower Brittany; to the east, Upper Brittany where Gallo is spoken. Overall, it has all the main characteristics of Armorica.

Côtes-du-Nord (literally "Coast of the North") - the emphasis is on the sea. Even more so in the unofficial name of "Côtes d'Armor". It's true that the coastline is the most active and most densely-populated region. The fertile alluvial plateaux gashed by deep estuaries (the Rance, Trieux and Jaudy) and the maritime climate are particularly favourable for animal farming and crops. This is the "golden belt". Fishing provides activity in numerous small harbours. It is, too, on these plateaux that you will find the main towns - Saint-Brieuc, Lannion, and Dinan. And tourism could scarcely have failed to develop along the Emerald and Pink Granite Coasts, both of them

superbly indented shorelines that have caused people to call Brittany "a masterpiece of the sea."

The uplands in the interior (the highest peak is Bel-Air, 1105 ft.) cross the département from west to east, extending Finistère's Monts d'Arrée. This is a watershed from which the Rance and other rivers flow down to the Channel. Apart from a few better-endowed basins like Loudéac, the Argoat is a poorer region and more isolated than the coast. And despite economic initiatives, it is being gradually eroded by a rural exodus. Yet this secretive part of Brittany, the land of hills and woodland, is steeped in beauty.

Along the coast in Le Val-André, a human tooth 200,000 years old was discovered! That will give you some idea of the length of the region's history. The Stone Age civilisation scattered menhirs and dolmens right across it. In Ancient Gaul, the Curiosolite and Osmismen tribes occupied an area corresponding to the dépar-

tement as we know it today. Rome imposed its own law on them. After three centuries of Gallo-Roman civilisation (cf. Corseul, the Little Pompei of Brittany), Armorica regained its Celtic character with the arrival of Britons from across the Channel who had fled the Saxon invasions. Led by their "patriot saints", Brieuc, Tugdual, Jacut, Guirec etc. they covered the area with the parishes whose names still begin with the typically Breton "plou" and "lan", even if the Celtic language has now receded beyond Saint-Brieuc.

In the 9th century, the Vikings arrived, bringing with them fire and mass slaughter. From the ashes of the kingdom of Brittany rose a new world - the feudal system. Great estates featured on maps of the day, areas like Penthièvre which stretched from R. Trieux to R. Rance. The Middle Ages had a far-reaching influence with St. Yves of Tréguier, St. Guillaume Pinchon of Saint-Brieuc, and the great abbeys like

3

Right : *the calvary at Kergrist-Moëlou.*

Bégard, Boquen and Beauport. But the towns (Dinan, Lamballe, Guingamp) acquired walls and ramparts to withstand attack during the War of Breton Succession (1341-1365).

There then followed a "golden century", the 15th century, under the peaceful reigns of dukes such as John V. The arts flourished, maritime trade expanded, and the canvas industry grew (Quintin, Uzel). After its annexation to France in 1532, Brittany's governor, Mercoeur, rebelled against the Protestant King Henri IV. During the reign of Louis XIV, there was the Red Bonnet Revolt involving the peasantry. The French Revolution brought about the creation of the département of Côtes-du-Nord, in 1790. Royalist insurrection was particularly rife in the Dinan, Lamballe and Moncontour neighbourhoods.

In the 19th century, Côtes-du-Nord was the most densely-populated département in Brittany.

But there were too many strong arms on the farms, no large ports, and few industries. During the Second Empire, the Paris-Brest railway was used by huge numbers of emigrants. After a century of stagnation made worse by two wars, the 1950's saw the beginning of an enormous modernisation programme. Farmers began working to European policies, though not without a number of crises, the fishing industry was updated, major roads made the region more accessible, and town planning was given priority. This was a profound change yet it has not made any essential difference to the beauty of the Breton countryside, as shown by the development of the tourist industry.

First there is the lively Trégor region - Tréguier (historically St. Yves' town), Lannion (the minor capital of the electronics industry), and Perros-Guirec and its beaches. The place where Renan, Le Braz, Luzel and many other writers and

artists once lived is still a hotbed of Breton culture.

Then comes the Goelo whose tall cliffs run from Paimpol, where memories of Icelandic fishermen are still very much alive, to Saint-Brieuc, the county town and the county's economic and cultural centre. Lamballe lies in the Penthièvre region bordered by the haughty shores of Cap Fréhel and Fort-la-Latte. Near the Rance is Dinan, one of the finest mediaeval towns in France.

From Guingamp to Rostrenen, you will be travelling in the Argoat, heading for Cornouaille with its sparkling bubbling rivers and streams. There are typical old villages, the "Little Switzerland" area round the Lac de Guerlédan, and countless churches, chapels and manorhouses, all of them expressions of an admirable popular art form.

Côtes-du-Nord is waiting to welcome you. Degemer mat !

The roodscreen in Loc-Envel.

BELLE-ISLE EN TERRE

Lying at the confluence of the rivers Léguer and Le Guic, 10 miles from Guingamp, this picturesque little town forms the gateway to the poetically Celtic woods known as **Coat-an-Hay** (the Day Forest) and **Coat-an-Noz** (the Night Forest). On the edge of the latter is the village of **Loc-Envel,** in the shadow of a remarkable 16th-century church. It has panelled vaulting decorated with painted hanging keystones, a very fine rood screen, a High Altar made of a single block of granite, a 17th-century reredos, and a stained glass window depicting the life of St.Envel.

Coat-an-Noz also contains the **19th-century castle** that once belonged to Lady Mond (1869-1949). What a romantic life for Maï Le Manac'h, the daughter of a modest miller from the forest. She married the extremely rich nickel king, Robert Mond. She then purchased the castle that had been so dear to her during her childhood. After having been left in ruins for years,

it is now undergoing restoration. Lady Mond, a great benefactress for the area where she was born, was buried in the crypt beneath the ossuary in **Locmaria's graveyard.** The village is a mile to the north of Belle-Isle. The chapel is attractive and has a 16th-century rood screen.

Five miles away is the **Beffou Forest** (yews and beech trees hundreds of years old). Just over five miles to the east is the calvary in **Gurunhuel,** which bears three crosses. The souls of the two thieves can be seen floating out their mouths. One of them is taken by an angel; the other one is carried off by a demon.

BOQUEN

Nestling in the depths of the forest near **Plénée-Jugon** (19 miles from Dinan), **Boquen Abbey** is a symbol of the spirit that never dies. Founded in 1137 by the Cistercians of Bégard, it prospered until the 15th century before falling into a decline. It was sold off during the French Revolution and used as a source of building stone. In 1936, Dom Alexis Presse,

who had been born locally, arrived from Tamié Abbey in Haute-Savoie "with no luggage other than a knapsack containing his breviary and a piece of bread". He was followed by three monks with whom he undertook to restore the abbey. One year later, it celebrated its 800th anniversary.

Since 1965, the 12th-century **minster** has regained all its original splendour. A magnificent set of rafters covers the vast 234 ft. nave supported by austere pillars with capitals and lit by tall semi-circular windows. The chancel dates from the 14th century and there is a stained glass window in the chevet. Other points of interest include the gravestone of Gilles of Brittany who was assassinated in 1450, the 12th-century chapter house, and the gallery in the cloisters (Romanesque capitals).

After the dissolution of the "Boquen Community" in 1976, a movement that had been led by Father Bernard Besret and whose ideas on the renovation of the Church had aroused severe controversy, the Order of Cîteaux gave the abbey to the Sisters of Bethlehem.

Le Port-Clos.

BRÉHAT

The pink island, the island of flowers. Painters and poets have vied with each other to honour the charm and attractions of Bréhat. "There is nothing to equal the splendour of the southern shores with their red rocks splashed with pine trees dipping their roots in a sea whose deep blue would be the envy of the Baie d'Antibes", wrote Charles Le Goffic.

The micro-climate is particularly appreciable, and aloes, oleanders, and palm trees all grow beside the harbour at **Port-Clos**. The average temperature in January is 6°C. Visitors are always struck by the mild climate when they arrive from the Pointe d'Arcouëst (10-minute crossing). The low houses and larger villas with luxurious gardens are a delight to the eye; they flank paths and narrow streets where cars are almost inexistent. There is silence.

This is a miniature world (2 miles long) of amazing diversity. Beyond the tiny village is **St.Michael's Chapel** on a hillock, and the **Maudez Cross**. Panoramic view of the island and the tumble of rocks along the shore. There is a bridge across the cove at La Corderie, a harbour used by the Newfoundland fishermen in 1504 and a haunt of privateers. The island's north coast is quite different - it is windswept moorland, and there are rocks at the **Peacock Lighthouse**

(Phare du Paon). At night, from the coastal station, you can see twelve lights sweeping across the sea.

A boat trip round the island gives a better picture of the coastline shredded into tiny islets - Béniguet, Ile Verte, Raguenez, Logodec etc. Saints from across the Channel who came here in the 5th century settled on some of them. In Maudez, there is still a round monk's cell with a roof in the shape of a turret. There are Gallo-Roman remains on Lavrec where Budoc founded the first Celtic monastery in Brittany.

More recent historical events have a less evangelical character. Bréhat was given fortifications and withstood the ravages of the One Hundred Years' War and the Wars of Religion, as well as the demands of the English, the Leaguers, and the Spaniards. In 1944, the Germans blew up the Paon and Rosedo Ligthouses. Today, Bréhat is a tranquil corner of paradise invaded only by tourists. It comes third to Mont Saint-Michel and Fréhel as the most popular place along the Channel coast.

Perros-Hamon Chapel in Ploubazlanec.

CALLAC

Callac on the borders of the Trégor and Cornouaille regions, is a major stock-breeding centre. In front of the stud stands the unexpected statue of - Naous the stallion. This is also the capital of the Breton spaniel.

The past has left some opulent reminders of Breton architecture and art in the modest villages nearby, in particular in **Bulat-Pestivien** (6 miles to the N). Its impressive church, once a much-visited place of pilgrimage, has the tallest tower in the département (215 ft). There is a wonderful Flamboyant Gothic porch whose central pillar is decorated with vines and statues of the apostles. The sacristy is decorated with pilasters and shells. Inside is the lord's gallery, an offertory table dating from 1553, and a lectern representing a young peasant. The graveyard contains a calvary and a well dating from 1718. The chapel and calvary in **Saint-Blaise en Pestivien** (17th century) are also worth a visit. The church in **Bur-turlet** dates from the 16th and 17th centuries.

Six miles from Callac is **Plourac'h** whose 14th-16th century church is known as the "cathedral of Argoat". It contains numerous statues, a 17th-century reredos, and a 16th-century Pietà. Pass through **Saint-Servais** where the town hall was the birthplace of the great Breton writer Anatole Le Braz (1859-1926) and go on to the **Duault Forest**. In the **Corong Gorge** the river disappears for a distance of 500

yds beneath an enormous pile of rocks. Two miles further on is **Locarn.** The church has a Passion Window (1572), a carillon drum, and a magnificent silver reliquary of St.Hernin in the presbytery.

CORSEUL

A set of Gallo-Roman remains that is unique in Brittany (6 miles from Dinan). Corseul, which was mentioned by Julius Caesar, was the capital of the Gallic Curiosolite tribe.

Conquered in 57 B.C., it took the name Fanum Martis. It was an important junction on the network of Roman roads for three hundred years, but was razed to the ground by the barbarians in 406 A.D.

A museum in the town hall contains numerous coins, items of pottery and miscellaneous objects. The neighbouring **Garden of Antiquities** contains the bases of a number of columns. In the church is the tombstone dedicated by the son of a woman called Sikilia Namgidde to

his mother; she had followed him from Africa to this far-distant garrison. The font supported by four figures dates from the 12th century.

The Champ-Malon dig is still providing new items of interest.

In the village of Haut-Bécherel on the Dinan road stand the impressive ruins of a 1st-century polygonal tower known as the **Temple of Mars.** A mile away, in the ruined castle of Montafilan, archaeologists discovered an altar dedicated to the Celtic goddess Sirona.

The Temple of Mars in Corseul.

DINAN

High above the deep fertile Rance Valley stand the tall ramparts of Dinan which visitors always find immediately attractive. It is one of the most beautiful, bright, mediaeval towns in Brittany. Emile Souvestre compared it to a "young girl trying on an old suit of armour over her ballgown".

Dinan (from the Celtic "dunum" meaning fortified upland) is a sub-prefecture with a population of 15,000 and its history is marked by siege upon siege. Its great man was **Du Guesclin** and as soon as you enter the town you will see his statue on the square that bears his name. On the neighbouring Place du Champ-Clos, the Constable challenged the English knight Thomas of Canterbury to a one-man fight during the siege of 1359.

You could easily spend hours just wandering through the labyrinth of tiny streets and squares flanked by timbered houses and houses with pillars forming porches. The **Rue de l'Horloge** is dominated by the 14th-century belfry with the slate steeple containing a bell that was a gift from Duchess Anne. The **Place des Merciers** is worth a visit for the picturesque inn called "Auberge de la Mère Pourcel" (16th century). Or you might take the Rue de l'Apport, the Place des Cordeliers where the vaulted gateway leads to a former 13th-century monastery that is now a high school, or the Rue de la Mettrie containing the birthplace of songster Théodore Botrel, or have a look at the Trinitarians' House (1368), the Keratry Mansion (now the Tourist Office), the Beaumanoir Mansion with its 16th-century gateway, or the 16th-century Plouer Mansion.

Top to bottom :

The harbour at Dinan.

Mediaeval houses.

The doorway of St.Saviour's Church.

The castle entrance.

St.Malo's Church (15th-19th centuries) has an ornate Renaissance chevet. Be sure not to miss St.Saviour's (église Saint-Sauveur) which has undergone much alteration but which still has a large number of Romanesque features. There is a magnificent 12th-century porch with three arches showing a blend of Romanesque, Byzantine and Persian architecture. There are bulls and winged lions, the symbols of St.Luke and St.Mark, above the tympanum. Inside, there is a Romanesque wall with blind arching on the right-hand side. The left side aisle is Gothic. The church also has a monumental High Altar with a canopy (18th century), a stained glass window depicting the Evangelists (15th century), a statue of Our Lady of Virtues (16th century) and a cenotaph containing Du Guesclin's heart.

Dinan also has a 14th-century castle comprising two towers, the Coetquen and the Duchess Anne (museum), connected by a curtain wall. Along the ramparts are fifteen towers and four gates. The moat has been made into parks, the Grands Fossés and Petits Fossés. From the English Garden behind St.Saviour's, there is a panoramic view of the R.Rance and the harbour. To reach the harbour, take the finest mediaeval street in Dinan, the Rue du Jerzual, which extends beyond the 13th-century Jerzual Gate into the Rue du Petit-Fort. The old houses, now turned into craft workshops, have been remarkably well-preserved e.g. the Governor's Residence in the Rue du Petit-Fort. From the harbour (Gothic bridge), you can take a trip along the R.Rance to the Chatelier Lock, Dinard and Saint-Malo.

One mile to the south is Léhon. The church still comprises a few features of the old St.Magloire's Abbey founded in the 9th century by Nomenoë. The 17th-century cloisters now lie in ruins. Above the village are the ruins of the feudal castle.

Dinan seen from Lanvallay.

15

Boats at their moorings in Erquy.

ERQUY

This is the foremost shellfish harbour in France and a very popular seaside resort in the lee of **Cap d'Erquy.** The area, with its tall red sandstone cliffs, was purchased by the département because of its geological, historical and ecological importance. There are a number of paths and roads across the moors, valleys and shore. Beyond the village of Tu-es-Roc are the remains of entrenchments called "Caesar's encampment", although they are doubtless older than the ancient "Reginea" which stood at the end of a Roman road.

Sables-d'Or-les-Pins, between Erquy and Fréhel, was totally man-made in 1924 and it enjoyed all the pomp and splendour of the "Roaring Twenties". There is a casino, the Palais des Arcades and a golf course. Elegant villas lie hidden amidst the pine trees.

Just over 3 miles from Erquy is the **Château de Bien-Assis.** Behind its 15th-century crenelated walls and moat is a fine 17th-century house.

Le Val-André, which was created in 1882 within the boundaries of Pléneuf, draws in large crowds of holidaymakers. The 2-mile beach is backed by a promenade and dyke. The Ile de Verdelet is a bird sanctuary. The tiny harbour of **Dahouet** still has all the picturesque charm of a long history. One mile away is the 14th-century St.James Chapel (Chapelle Saint-Jacques) with a lovely porch. It has retained all the mystery of a building that was never finished.

The harbour at Dahouët.

The Château de Bien-Assis.

FRÉHEL

This is one of the most grandiose spots anywhere in Brittany. Its sheer cliffs of shale, red sandstone and porphyry stand 227 ft. above the waves. It receives almost one million visitors every year.

It is from the sea (boats from Dinard and Saint-Malo) that the spot can be seen at its most impressive. The **lighthouse,** a square granite tower 315 ft. high with a range of 62 miles, was built in 1948 to replace the original, built in 1847 but destroyed by the Germans. Nearby is the old 18th-century lighthouse. In fine weather, from the platform of the main lighthouse, there is a vast panoramic view stretching from Bréhat to the Cherbourg Peninsula and Jersey.

The **Grande Fauconnière** at the tip of the headland is a nature reserve for thousands of birds. An amazing sight. There is also an abundance of flowers.

Across the Anse des Sévignés stands the haughty outline of the feudal **Fort-la-Latte,** 195ft. above sea-level. It had an eventful history with sieges in the 14th, 15th and 16th centuries. Louis XIV ordered the fort to be restored because it held a strategic position in the 17th century. In 1731, a marriage caused it to pass from the Gouyon-Matignon family to the Grimaldis of Monaco.

Built on a rocky islet connected to the mainland by two drawbridges spanning deep crevasses, La Latte still has its ring of ramparts and its towers, the guardroom, the inner residence, the chapel built in 1420, and the central keep on its motte. It is a unique piece of mediaeval scenery which has been used for many a swashbuckling film.

Cap Fréhel ▶

Fort-La-Latte.

The Abbey of Bon-Repos.

On previous pages : *the grandiose Fréhel promontory.*

GUERLÉDAN

The winding wooded banks of the **Guerlédan Lake** stretch over 14 miles in a hilly region on the borders of Côtes-du-Nord and Morbihan. It has a Vosgian-type beauty which has made it the top tourist attraction in Central Brittany.

The manmade lake came into being with the construction, between 1923 and 1929, of the hydroelectric dam (222 yds. long, 146 ft. high) which cut across the Nantes-Brest canal. The valley was flooded and given eighteen locks. Every ten years, the dam is drained, uncovering the lunar landscape of the drowned valley.

The departure point for a tour of the lake is the tiny town of **Mûr.** It has a Breton Neo-Gothic church dating from 1873, the 16th-century St.Suzanne's Chapel with a close filled with age-old beech trees that featured on a canvas by Corot. There is a marina on the lake. The N164 road leads to **Caurel** (leave the road at Beau-Rivage). Near Gouarec, turn right onto the Lanicat road. It runs through the **Daoulas** Gorge where a waterfall cascades down between peaks topped with jagged needles of shale. Back on the N164, you will find the **Abbaye de Bon-Repos** (Abbey of Rest) in a charming spot near an old bridge. All that remains of the Cistercian abbey founded in 1184 by Alain de Rohan are majestic 17th-century ruins covered in greenery. A restoration project is underway.

From the abbey head for the **hamlet of Les Forges** and the Fourneau (literally ''kiln'') Lake. The former site of a 17th-19th century ironworks still has well-preserved houses and other buildings as well as the forge foreman's house. Further on is the **Château des Salles,** the cradle of the Rohan family, on the banks of a lake.

Return to Mûr via the dense **Quénécan Forest** (2,500 hectares). Near the dam is an attractive 15th-century chapel, St.Trefine's. Don't leave Mûr without taking a trip along the Saint-Gilles-Vieux-Marché road through the **Poulancre Gorge.**

Sunset over Guerlédan.

The former Bégard Abbey.

GUINGAMP

Guingamp lying at the junction of the Armor and Argoat regions, is a sub-prefecture with a population of 10,000 and it has maintained its very Breton character, as shown by its Festival of Breton Dance, held on the third Sunday in August.

All that the town has to show for its eventful history as a fortress continually being captured and recaptured are a few stretches of rampart. The remainder were dismantled in 1626 on the orders of Cardinal Richelieu. On the Place du Centre are old granite houses and the fine Renaissance fountain called **La Plomée** (1588). It has three basins, one above the other, supported by rams' heads, dolphins and nymphs.

Notre-Dame de Bonsecours (Our Lady of Help) houses a Black Virgin which is the only one of its kind in Brittany. The chapel beneath the north porch sparkles with candles. There is a pilgrimage, night-time procession and fireworks display on the first Saturday in July. The basilica (12th-15th centuries) has a history of ups and downs. The American bombing raid of 7th August 1944 demolished the 13th-century steeple, which was rebuilt in 1956. In 1535, when one of the towers fell down, the entire south-western section of the building collapsed - hence the complex architectural styles. The south wall (Duke's Portal) and West Front (richly decorated doorway) form a stark contrast to the more austere north wall. Inside at the transept crossing, between slender pillars with flying buttresses, are four Romanesque arches.

The town hall is housed in the former Augustinian hospital convent.

There is a fine 17th-century façade with a forepart.

A mile away is the interesting Flamboyant Gothic church of **Grâces** (1506). It has some strange keystones illustrating the theme of drunkenness. The church also houses the relics of Charles of Blois, the unlucky pretender to the Duchy of Brittany who was killed at the Battle of Auray in 1364 and later proclaimed one of the Blest by the Roman Catholic Church. A mile to the south are the ruins of the Holy Cross Abbey (Sainte-Croix). Seven miles away is **Bourbriac** whose patron saint, Briac, has two tombs in the church - one dating from the 16th century and the other, a stone coffin, in the Romanesque crypt. Six miles to the south-east is the chapel of Avaugour (14th-15th centuries).

La Plomée Fountain in Guingamp.

town, the former castle chapel, now the Collegiate Church of Our Lady the All-Powerful (Notre-Dame de Toute-Puissance), has kept its massive appearance. There is a panoramic view from the terrace. The north porch is Romanesque with slender colonnettes topped with capitals, the chancel dates from the 14th century, the roodscreen is 15th century and the organ dates from the reign of Louis XIII. In St.Martin's (15th century), the Romanesque south porch has a carved wooden canopy. In St.John's (Eglise Saint-Jean), dating from the 15th-19th centuries, there are three wonderful reredos.

Among the old houses on the Place du Martray, the **Public Executioner's House** (16th century) contains not only the Tourist Office but also the Mathurin Méheut Museum. He was a painter well-known for his pictures of traditional Brittany. There is also the Old Lamballe Museum.

The County of Penthièvre was afforded further protection by the huge **Château de la Hunaudaie** (14th century) belonging to the great Tournemine family ("in Brittany, it is said that Monsieur de la Hunaudaie is only slightly less of a great lord than the king"). During the French Revolution, it was destroyed by the Republican forces in order to remove a Royalist rebel stronghold. It was purchased by the State and underwent restoration. With its jagged towers, the stumps of chimneys, its curtain walls and the Renaissance house, it still has an air of greatness in its solitary woodland.

Jugon, 6 miles to the south, also had a castle deemed to be impregnable. It was said that, "He who holds Brittany without holding Jugon has a head without a hood". The castle no longer exists but Jugon is a pleasant place to stay in the Arguenon Valley, on the banks of a 300-hectare lake.

LAMBALLE

Lamballe at the gateway to the beaches at Le Val-André and Erquy lies at the centre of a rich agricultural area. It has a large stud farm and is the former capital of the County of Penthièvre. It was a fortress beneath whose walls the famous one-armed Huguenot Captain "Ironarm" La Noue died in 1591. The Duchess of Lamballe, a friend of Marie-Antoinette, died in the 1792 massacres and her head was paraded through the streets of Paris on a pikestaff.

Richelieu had the castle and town walls demolished but, high above the

Lamballe : the roodscreen in St.John's Church.

Mathurin Méheut : "The fishing smack".

LANNION

This used to be one of those little towns "that seem to age without losing anything of their original gracefulness". Then, in the early 1960's, came the shock of modernity with the opening of the National Centre for Telecommunications Research (Centre National d'Etudes des Télécommunications) and the tracking station at Pleumeur-Bodou. The electronics industry soon followed. Lannion, a sub-prefecture with a population of 6,000, was three times larger than before.

The modern housing estates are still developing further afield, but the town centre has retained its Breton character. From the Quai d'Aiguillon on the banks of the R.Léguer, narrow streets lined with timbered houses and twisted gables lead up to the Place du Maréchal Leclerc. On the square are **two very fine houses** dating from the 15th and 16th centuries, one of them supported by caryatids and the other one entirely slatehung. Nearby, in the Rue Geoffroy de Pontblanc, a cross commemorates the heroic defence put up by the knight of the same name against the English invader in 1346.

The **Church of Saint-Jean-du-Baly** (16th-17th centuries) has a square tower and an organ dating from 1627 (a well-known music festival is held here every summer). Much more interesting, though, is **Brélevenez Church** which dominates the town from the top of 140 steps lined with flower-decked houses, a scene that is sure to catch an artist's eye. Its name, meaning "hill of joy" in Breton, is a reminder of the knights of Montjoie, part of the Order of the Knights Templar. There is a two-storey belltower with a 15th-century spire. The apse and porch are Romanesque ; the porch has six rows of arching topped by three colonettes. The nave is wood panelled and the pillars lean at odd angles. The 12th-century granite stoup was originally a corn measure. There are some fine reredos, a 15th-century stained glass window, and a crypt containing a statue of the Laying in the Tomb (18th century).

On the Perros-Guirec road stands the **CNET's Hertzian relay tower,** looking down on a complex of electronics research laboratories where tomorrow's techniques are developed, e.g. the Renan telephone

Old houses on the Place du Centre in Lannion.

system. There are also specialist factories.

The **Pleumeur-Bodou Satellite Tracking Station,** a strange enormous white dome in the midst of the moorland is the most popular tourist attraction in Brittany (2,500,000 visitors since 1962). Beneath its 162-foot high Dacron dome, it houses an impressive cone-shaped antenna weighing 340 tonnes. It stands 95ft. high and it picked up the first television picture from America on 11th July 1962. Technical progress led to the construction of seven huge external dish aerials round the dome. A planetarium is due to be opened soon.

THE LÉGUER

"In silence, you unfurl,
oh Léguer,
Your ribbon of black velvet".

A trip up Lannion's river described in song by the poetess Anjela Duval will take you past châteaux and chapels set amidst woods and thickets.

Near Ploubezre on the road south from Lannion to Plouaret are the impressive ruins of the **Château de Coatfrec,** lost in the depths of the forest. This was the haunt of Guy Eder de la Fontenelle, who terrorised Brittany in the 16th century when he swept through the Trégor region.

Take time to stop at the charming **Kerfons Chapel,** a gem of Flamboyant Gothic and Renaissance architecture nestling beneath beech trees. There is a magnificent 15th-century roodscreen with five arches and fifteen panels depicting saints and apostles.

The **Château de Tonquedec** stands on a spur of rock above the deep narrow valley. Its feudal ruins are among the largest in Brittany. It was demolished for the first time on the

The ruins of Tonquédec.

The Chapel of the Seven Saints.

orders of Duke John IV (1395), rebuilt in the 15th century, and again razed to the ground when Richelieu was in power. Its mighty walls surround an inner courtyard, an enormous well-preserved keep with walls 13 feet thick, and a corner tower. From the parapet walk, there is a panoramic view.

The walls of the **Château de Kergrist** (16th-18th centuries) show three different architectural styles. The oldest, with its turrets and tall sloping dormer windows, overlooks the main courtyard. A 17th-century façade stands behind a balustraded terrace. The third wall, with two towers and a staircase, opens onto the formal garden.

The **Chapelle des Sept Saints** (Chapel of the Seven Saints) in Vieux-Marché is dedicated to the Seven Sleepers of Ephesus, seven young people who were walled up alive on the orders of Emperor Decius in the 3rd century for having refused to deny their faith. They awoke two hundred years later. Rather strangely installed in Brittany, the cult shared by Islam and Christianity was the basis of a unique joint religious procession created in 1954 by the great Oriental scholar, Louis Massignon.

The 18th-century chapel was built over a crypt-dolmen. Statues of the seven saints stand above the altar. Nearby is the source of the R.Stiffel whose waters gush out of seven holes. The bell in the church in Vieux-Marché comes from the former cathedral in Algiers.

Vieux-Marché was the birthplace of the Breton poetess Anjela Duval (1905-1981) and the folklore expert Luzel (1831-1895), who collected countless tales and songs. March'arit Fulup, the illiterate peasant woman who gave him all the treasures stored in her vast memory, is commemorated in a statue in Pluzunet.

The Trieux Estuary.

storeys and an attic with tall chimneys, and the staircase tower has a pepper-pot roof. The parapet walk looks down on the R. Trieux. The castle was purchased by the département which organises cultural events there during the summer season.

Lézardrieux is the point of departure for a trip to the **"Wild Peninsula"** between the Trieux and Jaudy estuaries. In **Pleubian**, there is a 15th-century pulpit, the oldest one in Brittany. The parapet round the cross has carvings representing scenes from Christ's Passion.

The **Sillon de Talbert** is a geographical oddity. It is a narrow bank of sand and shingle formed by the currents of the Trieux and Jaudy flowing in opposite directions, and it juts two miles out into the sea towards the Les Heaux Lighthouse, the tallest seabound lighthouse in France (146 ft.). Efforts are being made to stop the Sillon breaking up because it protects the surrounding oyster farms. The coastline is parti-

The Château de la Roche-Jagu.

LÉZARDRIEUX

Halfway between Paimpol and Tréguier, the road crosses a suspension bridge 260 yds. long over **R. Trieux** at Lézardrieux, a marina and centre for oyster-farming. There is a splendid view of the river, which becomes an arm of the sea at high tide, in fact one of the most beautiful rias in Brittany.

In summer, a boat trip from l'Arcouest-Bréhat up the estuary is highly recommended. The river flows between wooded banks dotted with houses and villas. Beyond the bridge, it crosses the Lancerf Moors where Alain Barbe-Torte, the Liberator of Brittany, defeated the Vikings in 936 A.D.

The **Château de la Roche-Jagu** stands in a superb setting high above the valley. It can also be reached from the Lézardrieux-Pontrieux road. Built in the 15th century, it has all the characteristics of a "fortified residence", somewhat midway between fortress and manor. It has two

cularly rich in algae, which has led to the opening of an algae research institute in Larmor-Pleubian.

LOUDÉAC

This sleepy former subprefecture with its agricultural market was brought back to life by the food-processing industry, which has doubled its population to 10,000 since the war. Well-known horse races are held there and the local people stage a Passion Play every year. Loudéac itself is of no real interest to tourists (18th-century church with a High Altar topped by a gigantic canopy) but it has made its neighbourhood highly attractive, especially the extensive forest.

On the edge of the woodland is **Querrien,** famous for the pilgrimage to Notre-Dame de Toute-Aide (Our Lady of Assistance), which came into being after the Virgin Mary had appeared to a young deaf and dumb shepherdess, in 1652.

Eight miles away in **Le Quillio** is a parish close, a calvary with a Pietà, and numerous items of furniture from Bon-Repos. Six miles to the south-east is **La Chèze** (ruins of Lanthenac Abbey, and a Tool Museum). In **La Ferrière,** the church has Renaissance windows and a very fine 16th-century Virgin Mary of the Annunciation. **Merdrignac** (9 miles away) is popular as a rural tourist centre near the Hardouinais Forest.

The High Altar in Loudéac.

The chapel on the Méné-Bré.

MÉNÉ BRÉ

Méné Bré, a tall lonely mound of rock above the Trégor plateau between Guingamp and Belle-Isle-en-Terre, is considered as something of a mountain, hence its name. Yet it stands at only 981 ft. There is a vast panoramic view. "He who has looked at Brittany from the summit of Bré is sure to have a wonderful picture to take away with him", wrote Anatole Le Braz.

This sacred hill has a chapel dedicated to St.Hervé, a blind bard who lived in the 6th century. It is said that somewhere here, sleeping in the midst of his treasure trove, lies Gwench'lan, another blind bard and the enemy of the saint. This is also said to be the place where thirty bishops held a council to curse Conomor the tyrant. Occasionally, a priest would come here at midnight, barefoot, to say Mass backwards in an attempt to tear a soul away from the Devil.

People prayed to St.Hervé when suffering from scalp disorders, and he also provided protection against wolves (a wolf was his constant companion). Mothers would come here to bathe sick children in the spring that the saint caused to gush forth. He also protected horses, and the horse fairs on Méné-Bré were famous far afield.

Six miles to the north is the town of **Bégard** which grew up around its former Cistercian abbey, the oldest in Brittany, founded in 1130. All that remains of the "Little Cîteaux of Armorica" are the sections that were rebuilt in the 17th-19th centuries and that are now part of a psychiatric hospital.

MONCONTOUR

Although well off the beaten track, Moncontour is well worth a

The church in Trédaniel.

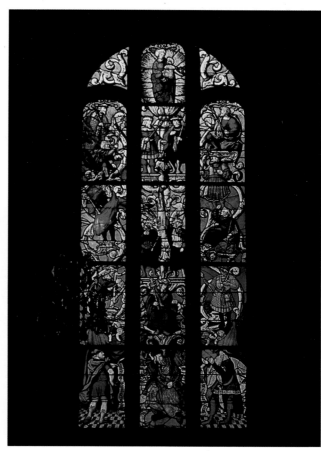

A stained glass window in Moncontour.

...isit. The former fortress of Penthiè-re standing on a spur of rock bet-...een two valleys was besieged on ...umerous occasions between the ...2th and 16th centuries. Richelieu ...rdered the ramparts to be demol-...shed. A few of the walls and gates ...re still upright, amidst the trees.

The town's prosperity was based ...n the canvas trade in the 18th cen-...ury. The last warlike event took ...lace during the French Revolution ...hen the Royalist rebels led by Bois-...ardy fought the Republican forces ...nder Hoche. All this past history ...eems to whisper in your ear as you ...troll along the tranquil hilly streets ...ned with old houses and granite ...ansions.

On the picturesque Place Penthiè-vre stands **St.Mathurin's Church** (a strange 16th-century belltower, 18th-century West Front), which has six stained glass windows inspired by Flemish art - some of the finest anywhere in Brittany. They depict Jesus as a child, St.John the Baptist, St.Barbara, St.Mathurin, St.Yves and a Rod of Jesse. There are numerous furnishings - reredos, organ loft, Pietà, and a marble High Altar dating from 1768. A religious procession is held on Whitsunday.

The **Château de la Touche-Trébry** lies 4 miles to the east. It has a feudal appearance (towers, moat, ramparts) but is, in fact, an elegant 16th-century residence.

The Chapel of **Notre-Dame in Haut-en-Trédaniel** (1 mile to the south) houses seven strange naive statues of saints who were able to cure ills - Yverdin and Eugenia (migraine), Houarnaule (phobias), Lubin (rhumatism), Hubert (rabies), Meen (insanity), and Mamert (colic).

Four miles to the east is **Bel-Air** (1105 ft), the highest point on the Méné. There is a 19th-century chapel. Eight radiating beech-lined avenues serve as a reminder of the ancient cult of sun worship (the name Bel Air comes from Belenos, the Celtic sun god). In fine weather, there is a vast panoramic view as far as the Baie de Saint-Brieuc.

PAIMPOL

In the land of the "Icelandic Fisherman", the schooners of yesteryear are no more than a memory. But Paimpol, which lost one hundred boats and 2,000 seamen between 1852 and 1935, remains profoundly affected by this period of its history. It is obvious whether you take a simple stroll along the jetties banked by shipowners' houses, a visit to the Maritime Museum, or a walk through the narrow streets and across the Place du Martray where one of the houses with a turret (16th century) was described in Pierre Loti's novel as the home of his hero, Gaud. Near the tower of the old church is a monument to Théodore Botrel, who wrote the song "La Pampolaise".

The maritime traditions have survived through inshore fishing, the coastal trade, and yachting but the closure of the National Merchant Navy College was a cruel blow. Paimpol, which enjoys a particularly mild climate, makes a living from early and late vegetables.

On the Bréhat road, there is a fine view of the bay from the Kerroc'h Tower. **Ploubazlanec**, where Loti's heroes lived, also commemmorates the "Icelandics" - the wall in the cemetery dedicated to those lost at sea, the votive offerings in the **Perros-Hamon Chapel,** and the Widows' Cross from which local women would search the horizon.

Boats for Bréhat leave from **l'Arcouest.** Marie Curie and Hélène and Frédéric Joliot-Curie used to spend the summer in this tiny village, which gained the nickname "Sorbonne Plage" (Sorbonne Beach). There is a superb panoramic view of the rugged coastline.

Three miles away is **Loguivy-de-la-Mer,** a small lobster-fshing port on the Trieux Estuary whose picturesque charms attract tourists and artists alike. Lenin spent some time here. There is a pretty Neo-Gothic chapel (1938).

The Kerroc'h Tower.

On the eastern outskirts of Paimpol at the head of the Kérity Cove is **Beauport Abbey,** majestic ruins draped in vegetation. Founded in 1202 by Alain de Penthièvre for the Premonstratensians from La Lucerne, it governed thirteen parishes in the Middle Ages. Later it became a place of decadence and was sold and abandoned during the French Revolution. It is now private property and its ruins have been shored up.

The tall vaulted minster was built in the Norman style and although it now stands open to the sky and its tombs are hidden among the hydrangeas, it is still very attractive. There is a chapter house, a refectory with windows overlooking the sea, the remains of the cloisters, the vaulted Duke's Chamber, and the cellars.

Go on to Plouézec and from there turn onto the Port-Lazo road and the **Pointe de Bihit** (panoramic view of the bay at Paimpol). There is also a delightful view from the **Pointe de Minard** (2 1/2 m. to the east).

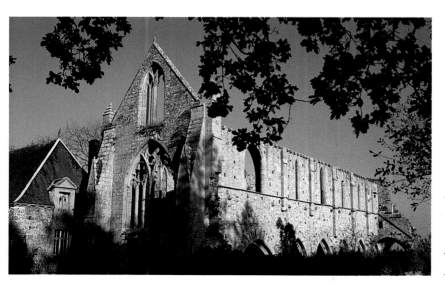

Top to bottom :

The harbour at Paimpol

Votive offerings from Newfoundland fishermen in Ploubazlanec.

Beauport Abbey.

35

Trestraou Beach.

Opposite, top to bottom : ,
Fishing boats and pleasure craft in Perros-Guirec.

Strange-shaped rocks in Trégastel.

PERROS-GUIREC

At the western end of the Trégor region, is the **Pink Granite Coast,** an outstanding natural setting for the development of one of the largest tourist complexes anywhere in Brittany.

Perros-Guirec has been the best-known of all the seaside resorts since it was first created in 1885. There are three centres of activity. At sea level, there is the bay, the fishing port and the yachting marina that is the starting point for major races during the summer months. Up the hill is the shopping centre around **St.James' Church** (église Saint-Jacques). It has a square 14th-century pink granite tower with a balustrade, a 17th-century dome, and a bell turret. The Romanesque south porch has four rows of coving and a tympanum. The Romanesque nave with its mas-

The Saint-Duzec menhir.

In Saint-Samson.

sive pillars and capitals illustrating scenes from the Bible is extended by the Gothic chancel. There is a granite stoup (17th century), and a very fine three-storey reredos (17th century).

Now for the beaches. **Trestignel** nestles in the lee of the Pointe du Château and the long Island of Tomé. The great painter Maurice Denis used to live in the villa called "Silentio", from which he admired what he himself described as "the most beautiful piece of scenery in the world". There is an orientation table on the cliff road. The road then runs down to the main beach at **Trestraou** (casino, Conference Centre, thalassotherapy institute). This is the pride and joy of Perros.

From Trestraou, a cliff walk four miles long leads to Ploumanac'h, passing some magnificent rocky landscapes on the way. Offshore are the Sept Iles looking like "a group of prehistoric mammals playing on the horizon", according to Anatole Le Braz. The best-known of the islands is Rouzic, the largest seabird reserve in France (shags, gannets, puffins, guillemots, kittiwakes, and herring gulls). The island's population has now gained strength again, after the mass murders of the major oil slicks. Chicks had to be imported from the Faroes.

Visitors cannot land on Rouzic, or on any of the other islands (Bono, Malban etc.). The boats only stop at the Ile aux Moines, once inhabited

by Franciscan friars. There is a lighthouse and an 18th-century fortress.

On the Perros-Ploumanac'h road, a stop at the **Chapelle de la Clarté** (Chapel of Light) is a "must". The chapel is said to have been built in accordance with a vow made by the lord of Barac'h. He was shipwrecked and he promised to build a chapel wherever land could be sighted through the mist. It is an attractively decorated building of pink granite with a square tower, a 17th-century spire, and a south porch with a carved wooden grille and a lintel. The statue of Our Lady of Light (to whom people pray when suffering from eye disorders) is carried in procession during the religious festival held on 15th August. In La Clarté, the pink granite quarries are also worth a visit. The stone has been used for numerous monuments, including the Cross of Lorraine at Colombey.

Ploumanac'h, once a fishing hamlet, nestles between enormous rocks with odd shapes such the one on the **Saint-Guirec Beach** known as "Napoleon's hat". It seems to be about to tumble over yet it has stood there for thousands of years, despite constant erosion. Nearby is the Saint-Guirec shrine in which young women who have not found a husband stick a needle in the saint's nose. High above the pile of granite rocks is the Neo-feudal Château de Coastaères (19th century) where the Polish writer Sienkiewicz is said to have written "Quo Vadis". From Saint-Guirec, there is a footpath to the coastal station and the Squewel Park which contains some superb rocks. Near the harbour is the Vallée des Traouieros, spanned by the road. It is an inextricable muddle of rocks and vegetation.

Trégastel is quite the equal of Ploumanac'h for its odd rocks, like the Thimble on the Coz-Pors Beach or King Gradlon's Crown at the Grève Blanche. Near Coz-Pors is the popular statue of the Eternal Father, on a pile of rocks housing a marine aquarium and an archaeological museum. From the statue, there is a lovely walk to the Ile Renote, which despite its name is really a peninsula.

In **Trégastel-Bourg,** the semi-Romanesque St.Anne's Church (12th-13th centuries) with its adjoining ossuary (17th century) has a traceried gallery and a lantern dome. It is a tranquil place, the burial ground of the poet and novelist Charles Le Goffic (1863-1932) whose works all centre on Brittany. Half-a-mile from the village are the Kergantuil dolmen and passage grave.

The corniche, or coast road, runs on down to Trébeurden.

Taking care of the nets...

PLOUHA

This large village, which lies on the borders of the Breton and French speaking areas of Brittany, is surrounded by places of interest. Two miles away is the **Chapel of Kermaria-an-Isquit** (literally, "the house of Mary who cures ills") dating from the 13th century. It is famous for its striking danse macabre showing 47 characters from right across mediaeval society, from the Emperor down to a labourer, being led by skeletons in an infernal saraband. Legends in Gothic script underline the precariousness of things on earth (e.g. "even the richest has nothing but a shroud").

Half-a-mile from Pléhédel is the **Lanleff "temple"**, for many years a source of intrigue for archaeologists. Gallo-Roman? Merovingian? In fact, it is an 11th-century Romanesque chapel built to the same layout as the Holy Sepulchre. The nave in the shape of a rotunda is flanked by a circular ambulatory with twelve arches and the capitals bear some very primitive carvings. The difference between this building and the elegant Renaissance chapel in **Tréméven** (1542) two miles away is quite striking.

Three miles to the north of Plouha is **Lanloup Church**, with a 16th-century Flamboyant Gothic porch decorated with numerous statues. The great composer Guy Ropartz (1864-1955) is buried in this village.

Bréhec, a notch in a coastline where the cliffs stand 325 ft. high, is a small harbour and a sheltered beach. This is said to be the place where St. Brieuc and the first immigrants from Britain landed in the 5th century. History leaps 1500 years at the cove in Cochat (codenamed "**Bonaparte Beach**"). It was here that 135 airmen and allied agents boarded ship and set sail for England during the dark nights of 1944. The Shelburne network took them as far as "Alphonse's house". Colonel Rémy's account is worth reading.

Bonaparte Beach.

Statues of the apostles in the porch.

The Danse Macabre in Kermaria-an-Isquit.

The temple in Lanleff.

PONTRIEUX

The tides roll far inland along the Breton estuaries. Because of this, Pontrieux on the R.Trieux, over 12 miles from the coast, is the second-largest port in the département after Le Légué thanks to the sand trade. The small town of old houses has a certain charm with its 18th-century granite fountain opposite the church of Notre-Dame des Fontaines. There is a "pardon" (religious procession) with an evening procession in July.

Pontrieux is a good centre from which to tour the inland Trégor region. In addition to the La Roche-Jagu (cf.Lézardrieux), visitors should be sure to see the outstanding parish close at Runan (3 miles away). It belonged to the Knights Templars and, later, to the Knights Hospitallers of St.John of Jerusalem, and was substantially patronised by Duke John V. The south wall is Flamboyant Gothic and has a porch bearing a coat-of-arms with coving and statues of the apostles, topped by a lintel. There is a Renaissance ossuary. Inside, there is woodpanelling and painted keystones, a reredos made of blue Tournai stone (1421), and a stained glass window depicting the Crucifixion. Outside is a polygonal calvary-pulpit bearing three Crosses.

La Roche-Derrien in the delightful Jaudy valley is just over 3 miles away. It was once a town of flax scutchers and itinerant rag merchants. As a fortress, it was the scene of bitter struggles between the French and English in the 14th century. Charles of Blois was wounded there and taken prisoner in 1367. The castle was razed to the ground and a 17th-18th century chapel now stands on the site. On the Place du Martray, there are old timbered houses. The church is Romanesque and Gothic (south porch dating from the 15th century, High Altar and very ornate reredos, organ from Westminster). In Berhet (8 miles to the south) is the interesting Chapelle de Confort (16th century).

Pontrieux : the fountain.

Runan Church.

QUINTIN

This small lakeside town exudes an elegant charm. As a prosperous canvas town in the 17th and 18th centuries, it acquired some fine old houses and granite mansions on the Place du Martray and the Place de 1830.

The **17th-century castle** has never been completed. Henriette de la Tour d'Auvergne, who had commissioned the original house in 1645, had to interrupt the work on the King's orders - in high circles, it was feared that the place might turn into a Pro-

The castle at Quintin.

testant stronghold. The other buildings date from 1775.

Notre-Dame Basilica has a statue of Our Lady of Deliverance in the porch. Women in labour would pray to Her. People also venerate the Virgin Mary's belt here; it was brought back from the Crusades by a lord of Quintin and it miraculously escaped the fire in 1600.

Nearby are castles and manorhouses that bear witness to the region's wealthy past. Among them are the **Château de Robien** (a mile to the south) and, six miles to the south, in L'Hermitage, the huge **Château de Lorge** near the delightful forest of the same name. Three miles to the south is **Uzel,** once the centre of the canvas trade, and the birthplace of Fulgence Bienvenue, the designer of the Paris Underground (1852-1936).

ROPHÉMEL

The R.Rance, which rises in the hills of the Méné region to the south of Moncontour, is dammed at Rophémel not far from Caulnes. The reservoir, which provides drinking water for Rennes, has added yet another beauty spot to a picturesque region where Royalist rebels were once legion. Near the lake is the 15th-century **Château de Beaumont.** In Caulnes, there is the 17th-19th century Couelan, which has a large Classical façade. In Le Quiou, on the Evran road, stands the well-preserved **Château du Hac** (14th century). In Evran, **Beaumanoir** (1628) is worth a visit.

There are also numerous old churches e.g. **Yvignac** 5 miles north of Caulnes. In a building that underwent alteration in the 19th century is an 11th-century Romanesque nave with massive square pillars and carved capitals. The doorway has arching. Yvignac is near Broons where Du Guesclin was born in 1320. A column on the edge of the RN12 road marks the site of the family manorhouse, which no longer exists.

Rostrenen :
Our Lady of the Thorn Bush.

ROSTRENEN

This is a very Breton town in the land of "festou-noz" (ceilidhs) and the "fisel" dance. The 16th-century collegiate church of Our Lady of the Thorn Bush (Notre-Dame du Roncier) originated in the discovery, in 1295, of a statue of the Virgin Mary hidden in a thorn bush which was flowering in the middle of winter. The porch is Gothic and Renaissance. There is a sacred well.

The entire Upper Cornouaille region is rich in beauty spots, churches, chapels, and manorhouses. In **Glomel** (5 miles away) the Nantes-Brest Canal crosses the highest point on its course (598 ft.) through a cutting 70 ft. deep dug by convicts between 1823 and 1836. A series of 44 locks leads to Carhaix, 11 miles away. The vast lake at Glomel has been laid out as a reservoir on the canal reach. Water sports are permitted.

Five miles away is the impressive parish close at **Kergrist-Moélou** - a very ornate Flamboyant Gothic church. Fine porch with statues of the apostles. Large calvary dating from 1578 but damaged during the French Revolution.

Nine miles from Rostrenen is another parish close, in **Lanrivain** (ossuary and calvary). Half-a-mile away is the chapel of **Notre-Dame du Guiaudet** (17th century) containing a statue of the Virgin Mary lying down with the Child Jesus. In **Trémargat**, a mile away, the R.Blavet disappears beneath the **Toul Goulic Rocks** and resurfaces some 500 yds. further on. **Saint-Nicolas-du-Pélem,** a centre of rural tourism, boasts a polychrome carillon drum in the Chapel of Notre-Dame du Ruellou (18th century).

The well in the church.

SAINT-BRIEUC

At the head of its vast triangular bay, the county town of Côtes-du-Nord lies at the geographical centre of the département. It is in a particularly good position on a plateau, between the deep Gouët and Gouédic valleys that are spanned by viaducts. The suburbs spread far afield, forming a town with a population of 100,000.

Saint-Brieuc got its name from a Welsh monk who came across the Channel in the 6th century. Miracles occurred on his grave, a pilgrimage began, and soon a town grew up on the site. In the 13th century, another great man came on the scene - Bishop **Guillaume Pinchon** who became the first official Breton saint when he was canonised in 1247. He defended his town against Duke Pierre Mauclerc. The cathedral became a fortress and was besieged by John IV in 1375, set alight by Olivier de Clisson in 1395, and ravaged by the wars of the League in the 16th century. The "Kindly City" was then to live in peace until the French Revolution. It was then renamed Port-Brieuc, and it fell into the hands of the Royalist rebels after a surprise attack in 1799; the rebels murdered the former parliamentarian Poulain-Corbion. In the 19th century, the harbour at Le Légué underwent expansion and the first industries appeared. Today, the town has a metalworks, a brush-factory, food-processing plants, and large-scale commercial and tertiary sector employment.

"Saint-Brieuc. Nothing", noted Flaubert, unfairly. It's true that this is no town of special architectural or artistic interest, but the **cathedral** is worth a visit; it has two towers bristling like a keep with slit windows

The Baie de Saint-Brieuc.

48

Saint-Brieuc Cathedral.

In the old town.

and machicolations. Inside, it is built in a composite style (12th-15th centuries). Items of interest include tombs, including that of St.Guillaume Pinchon, an organ dated 1540, a remarkable reredos in the Annunciation Chapel (15th century) and the stained glass window in the south arm of the transept (15th century).

Of the old town of Saint-Brieuc, which has been somewhat diminished by modern town planning, there remains the **La Grille District** not far from the cathedral where the streets are narrow and winding (Fardel, Quinquaine etc.) and the house fronts of a venerable age (15th-century Le Ribault House, former Residence of the Dukes of Brittany dating from the 16th century). In the Rue Notre-Dame, the Saint-Brieuc fountain sheltered by an attractive Gothic porch marks the site of the saint's first private chapel.

The Rue Saint-Guillaume is also worth a visit - it is the main street in the pedestrian precinct. And the **Grandes Promenades** park and statues are interesting. From the Aube and Huguin hills (where there is a monument to Anatole Le Braz) there are views of the town and the bay. Note the Côtes-du-Nord History Museum.

Saint-Brieuc was the birthplace of two great writers - Villiers-de-l'Isle Adam (1838-1889), author of the *Cruel Tales,* and Louis Guillou (1899-1980), the novelist who wrote *La Maison du Peuple* and *Jeu de patience,* describing his home town.

SAINT-CAST-LE-GUILDO

This is one of the gems of the Emerald Coast. Backed by the Boulevard de la Mer, the main beach forms a one-mile semi-circle between the **Pointe de la Garde** and the **Pointe de Saint-Cast**. In La Garde is a statue of Our Lady of La Garde by Armel Beaufils, which looks out onto a superb panoramic view. There is another splendid view from the Pointe de Saint-Cast where there is a coastal station, an orientation table, a monument to those who escaped from Nazi-occupied France and to the victims of the frigate "Laplace" which blew up on a mine in 1950.

Near the village a pillar topped by the statue of a greyhound slaughtering a leopard serves as a reminder of the **Battle of 1758.** A British force some 10,000 strong that had been landed in Brittany tried to return to the fleet moored off Saint-Cast. The force was routed by the Duke d'Aiguillon's troops. But the Duke had followed the battle from a mill where he spent his time flirting with the miller's wife. This caused La Chalotais, Advocate General to Brittany's Assizes to say that "the

The harbour at l'Isle-Saint-Cast.

French army covered itself in glory and the Duke in flour''. It is said that the victory was also due to Celtic fraternity; a detachment of Welsh soldiers who heard the Bretons singing in the same language as they spoke themselves laid down their arms.

Le Guildo lies in a delightful spot at the mouth of the Arguenon. The romantic ruins of the **castle** are filled with memories of Gilles de Bretagne who led a joyous life there with his English friends, hence perhaps the expression ''courir le guilledou'' (''to play the field''). Gilles was suspected of treason by his brother, Duke François II, and arrested. He was strangled in 1450.

On the bank opposite the castle is a natural item of interest : the ''ringing stones'' which produce a strange metallic clang when knocked together.

Three miles to the south is **Plancoët,** a pleasant little town on the R.Arguenon, famous for its mineral water. Chateaubriand spent his childhood holidays there with his grandmother, Madame de Bedée. ''If ever I have seen happiness,'' he wrote, ''it was certainly in that house''.

And back to the coast with **Saint-Jacut-de-la-Mer,** a long peninsula (beaches, fishing harbour) with the Pointe du Chevet at its tip. There is a good view of the Ile des Ebihens and the shoreline from Lancieux to Saint-Briac.

SAINT-MICHEL-EN-GRÈVE

Between Lannion and Morlaix stands the church of Saint-Michel-en-Grève and its maritime cemetery, overlooking a vast bay some three miles long - **Lieue de Grève.** The sea flows out to a distance of over a mile. Horse racing is held here.

Top to bottom :

Brittany : "the land of the setting sun".

The Château de Rosanbo.

Saint-Michel-en-Grève.

It was here that **St.Efflam** is said to have landed in 580 A.D., when he arrived from Ireland. Memories of the saint can be found everywhere. One of the villages bears his name (chapel and well). It is said to have been from the top of the 260-foot Great Rock that he forced a terrible dragon to throw itself down into the waves. In **Plestin**, St.Efflam's Church, with its triple porch dating from the 16th century, contains his tomb and his statue, as well as the statue of his very chaste wife, Enora.

Between Saint-Efflam and Plestin is the **Corniche de l'Armorique,** the coast road from which there are superb views of the Baie de Locquirec. The R.Douron marking the border between Côtes-du-Nord and Finistère flows into the bay. Toul-an-Hery is a picturesque harbour.

The hinterland is a mysterious part of the Trégor region, a place well worth discovering. Almost three miles from Saint-Michel is **Ploumi-liau Church** (1608), which has a striking statue of a skeleton holding a sickle - Ankou, the Breton incarnation of Death. Take the Yar Valley to visit the fine Renaissance churches at **Trémel, Plouzelambre,** and **Lanvellec** which has an outstanding organ built by the English master Robert Dallam in 1653 (mediaeval music concerts).

St.Nicholas' Chapel in **Plufur** (1495), lost in the midst of trees and shrubs, is a masterpiece of the Beaumanoir architecture that is so prevalent in the area - a belltower-wall flanked by a turret, and a three-sided chevet with traceried gables.

The **Château de Rosanbo** near Lanvellec features every architectural style from the 14th to the 19th century. In the formal gardens, there are arbours laid out by Le Nôtre. The château contains some remarkble 17th- and 18th-century furniture, Aubusson tapestries, and a library of 8,000 books built for Claude Le Pelletier, Colbert's successor.

SAINT-QUAY-PORTRIEUX

This is the largest seaside resort (five beaches) on the Goëlo coast between Saint-Brieuc and Paimpol. "Seabathing" was launched here in 1841 by two patients of a doctor practising in Guingamp ; they stayed in a convent. Today, hotels and villas stretch from the harbour at Portrieux (fishing, yachting) to the Pointe de Saint-Quay (coastal station, panoramic view of the Baie de Saint-Brieuc). A cliff path along the coast also provides some fine views.

Adjoining the south side of Saint-Quay is **Étables** with its two family

The Lieue de Grève.

Saint-Quay-Portrieux.

beaches of Le Moulin and Les Godelins. Then comes **Binic.** It is a bustling fishing harbour at the mouth of the R.Ic, and as far back as 1612 it was sending boats to Newfoundland. There are beaches, a Local History Museum and a Maritime Museum.

Three miles away in **Lantic** is the Chapel of **Notre-Dame de la Cour** (1440) which has stone vaulting. The chapel includes a wonderful stained glass window depicting the life of the Virgin Mary with characters wearing the costume of the 15th century. Six miles away is **Châtelaudren,** the former capital of the Goëlo region. The **Chapel of Notre-Dame du Tertre**

(14th-16th centuries) is famous for a very rare set of 132 painted panels decorating the vaulted roof in the chancel and St.Margaret's Chapel. There is a magnificent 17th-century gilded wood reredos and an alabaster statue of the Virgin Mary (15th century).

TRÉBEURDEN

At the end of the Corniche Bretonne (coast road), lies Trébeurden whose beaches,e.g. Tresmeur, are well sheltered. Porz-Mabo even lies due south. From the Pointe de Bihit,

there is a vast panoramic view stretching as far as Roscoff.

At low tide, the rocky wooded Le Castel hill leads to the **Ile Milliau.** The former Prime Minister, Aristide Briand, used to spend his holidays here. Now the island has a preservation order on it and has been restored because of its historical and ecological interest (passage grave).

Three miles to the north is **Ile Grande,** connected to the mainland by a causeway. Its famous blue granite has paved roads in the north of France and the Boulevard Haussmann in Paris. There is a bird sanctuary here. In the vicinity, emerging

from piles of rocks, are a few tiny islands e.g. Aval. The legendary King Arthur is said to lie sleeping under one of the neighbourhood's many megaliths, waiting for the Celts to call him...

Half-a-mile from the Penvern crossroads, on the Pleumeur-Bodou road, stands the **Saint-Duzec menhir** which is 26 ft. high. It was made Christian in the 18th century and now bears engravings of the symbols of Christ's Passion. It has a Cross at the top.

TRÉGUIER

If you're looking for the old, mysterious Brittany, then you'll find it in Tréguier, the country of ''Mr.St.Yves'', in the shade of the magnificent cathedral. Another saint, though, was the founder of the town - **Tugdual,** one of the seven ''founding saints'' of Brittany. He came from across the Channel in the 6th century and established a monastery on a hill above the rivers Jaudy and Guindy, which join forces in a vast estuary. Hence the Breton name ''Landreger'', the monastery of the three rivers.

It was in Minihy-Tréguier, half a league away, that **Yves Heloury (1253-1303)** was born, at the Kermar-

tin Manor. After studying theology and law in Paris and Orléans, he returned to his birthplace as Official (ecclesiastical judge) of Tréguier and Rector of Trédrez and Louannec. He showed immense charity in the service of the greatest possible spirit of justice. In 1347, he was canonised. He is the most universal of all Brittany's saints - protector of the poor, and patron saint of the legal profession. During the May procession,

barristers from all over the world escort the saint's head in procession to Minihy, where the 15th-century church was built on the site of the chapel founded by St.Yves.

On the **Place du Martray** bordered by timbered houses stands the cathedral, striking in its might and its verticality. Of the former Romanesque church built in the 10th century, all that remains is the Hastings Tower behind the 14th-century Sanctus Tower, and the central tower with the 205 ft. spire. In the Flamboyant Gothic south wall is the People's Porch, a veritable piece of lacework in stone, and the Bell Porch where the coving bears 40 statues. The third porch, and the oldest, is on the west side. The view down the slender

St.Yves' ''head''.

three-storey nave is admirable, as is the chancel with 46 Renaissance stalls, the 17th-century organ, and the statues including the one depicting St.Yves standing between a rich man and a pauper. In the centre of the cathedral is the venerated tomb of the saint (1886), an over-ornate copy of the one that was destroyed during the French Revolution. More austere is the modern John V's tomb in the Duke's Chapel.

There are wonderful **cloisters,** with 48 radiating arches "from which," writes Henri Queffelec, "you can see the mysterious upsurge of the cathedral rise transfigured". **Ernest Renan** would like to have been buried there. But that was an impossible wish for Tréguier's other famous son (1823-1892). He, too, left the town of his birth to study theology in Paris, like Yves Heloury, but he lost his faith there and became a leading figure among 19th-century philosophers. In 1903, the inauguration opposite the cathedral of a statue commemmorating the author of *The Life of Jesus* caused a riot in deeply-Catholic Brittany - and the construction of a Cross near the harbour in reparation for the wrong done. Passions then died down. Renan is little read these days except for his delicate *Memories of Childhood* which come alive in a visit to his birthplace, now a museum.

The names of the narrow sloping streets are reminders of the episcopal town of days long gone - le Vieil Evêché (Old Bishop's Palace), la Psalette (choir school), la Chantrerie (chantry), l'Hôtel-Dieu (hospital). The seminary is now a high school and the Bishop's Palace is now the town hall, the see having been abolished in 1801. A plate reminds passers-by that Tréguier was one of the earliest centres of printing in Brittany (1485). Opposite is a moving war memorial by Francis Renaud - a local woman wearing a mourning cloak.

In the Bois du Poète lies Anatole Le Braz (1859-1926), the "son of the mountains adopted by the sea". It was in **Port-Blanc** (6 miles away) that he gathered his *Legend of Death*. A charming beauty spot (16th-century chapel) that has attracted large num-

bers of writers and artists e.g. Botrel, Alexis Carrel who wrote **Man, the Unknown** in the Ile Saint-Gildas where he is buried, and the American aviator Lindbergh on the Ile d'Illiec. Jean Guéhenno wanted his ashes to be scattered at sea.

A local saying has it that there's "Paradise in Port Blanc, Hell in **Plougescrant".** Hell on this shore, which is jagged and indented like

none other, is a notch of rocks where the sea bubbles and froths. The **St.Gonery Chapel** is worth a visit. Its strangely-sloping tower may remind you of the leaning tower of Pisa; the interior is a rustic Sixtine Chapel. The wooden ceiling is covered with naive 15th-century frescoes illustrating Genesis and the New Testament. There is a calvary-pulpit in the parish close, topped by three Crosses.

Opposite : *the nave of Tréguier Cathedral.*

The chapel at Port-Blanc.

LE YAUDET

The Heather Coast (Côte des Bruyères) follows the Pink Granite Coast beyond the mouth of the R.Léguer. From Lannion, head for **Loguivy** (a mile to the south) and its charming parish close. There is a monumental Flamboyant Gothic gateway, and a Renaissance well with a wide basin (1573). Another, smaller well bears the statue of the saint who came from Ireland in the 7th century. The 15th-century church with its outside staircase leading up to the belltower contains numerous statues and a fine reredos of the Adoration of the Magi (17th century).

Le Yaudet, high above the mouth of the Léguer (the name means "old town" in Celtic), is a very old site which has not yet revealed all its secrets. The Gallo-Roman period left a few remains. It was a bishopric, briefly, in the 6th century. The town is said to have been destroyed by the Vikings in the 9th century. Legends also speak of Lexobia, a sunken town. In the strange church is a statue of the Virgin Mary lying on a bed of lace with the child Jesus, watched over by St.Joseph. Above them is the dove of the Holy Trinity.

In **Locquemeau,** there is a fishing harbour and a 16th-century church. The Pointe de Dourven and Pointe de Sehar are picturesque spots. Just over two miles away is **Trédrez,** where St.Yves was rector of the parish. The 16th-century church is of major interest - chevet with three pointed gables, porch with statues of the apostles, and ossuary. Inside is a statue of the Virgin Mary and a Rod of Jesse. The baptistery has a carved wooden canopy.

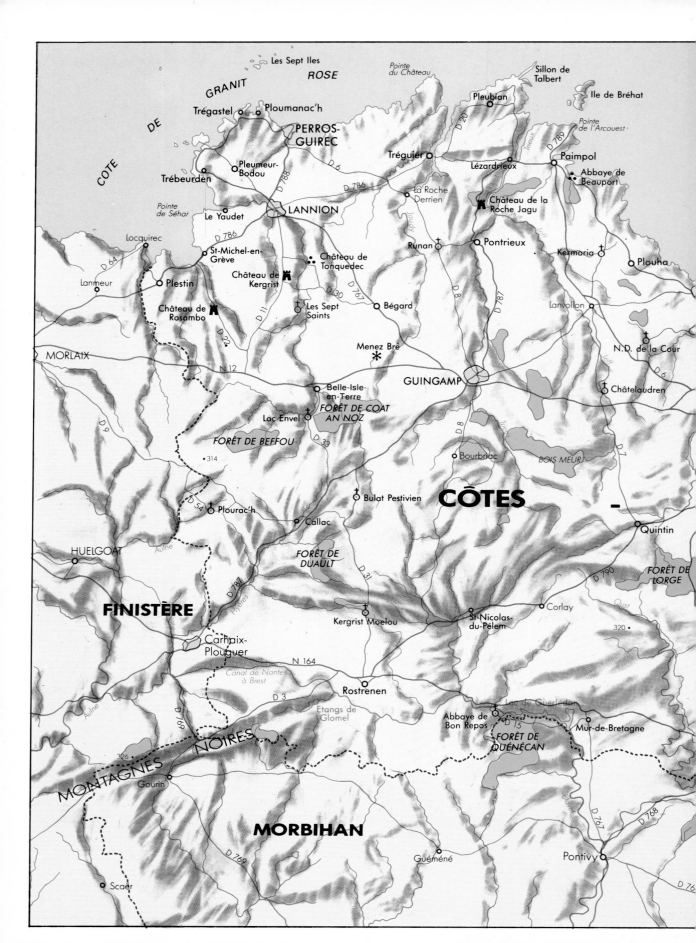

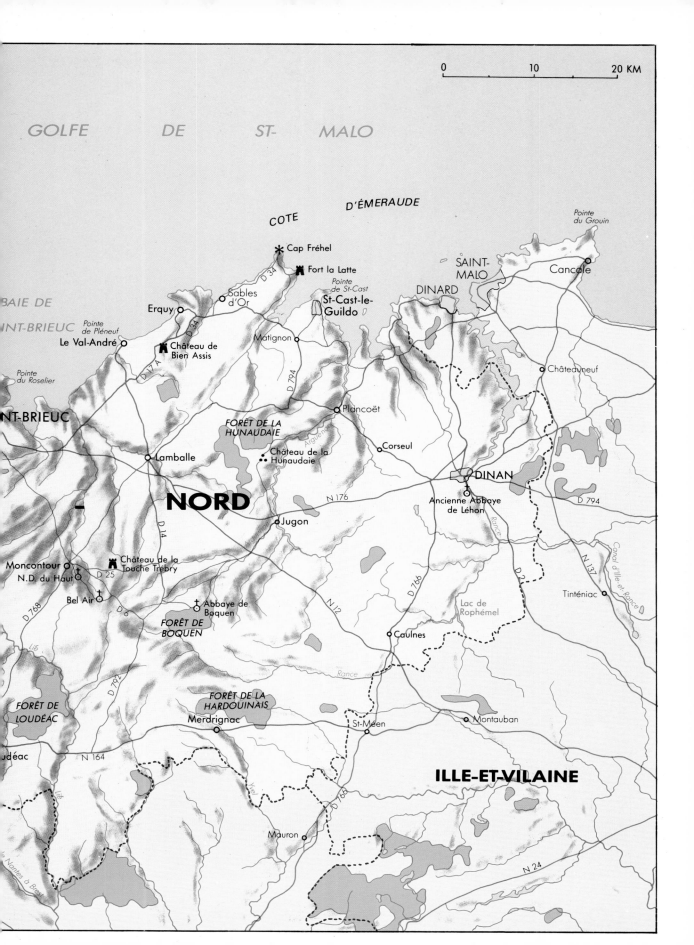

Armor : fishing smacks in Paimpol.

Argoat : the Toul Goulic Gorge.

PHOTOGRAPHIC CREDITS

Hervé Boulé : p. 17, 19, 50, 52 (*top*), 55, 56.

Hervé Champollion : p. 20, 21, 43.

Philippe Cherel : p. 4.

Louis-Claude Duchesne : p. 28.

Nicolas Fediaevsky : p. 6, 12, 14, 25, 26, 31, 33, 37, 38, 44 (*bottom*), 57.

Michel Ogier : p. 2, 3, 5, 10, 11, 16, 18, 22, 23, 24, 29, 30, 32, 34, 35 (*centre*), 36 (*top*), 39, 40, 41, 42, 44 (*top*), 45, 46, 47, 48, 49, 51, 52 (*centre and bottom*), 53, 54, 60,61.

Philippe Thomas : p. 7, 8, 9, 13, 17.

G. Vicaire : p. 36 (*bottom*).

BIBLIOGRAPHY

Histoire de Bretagne, Durtelle de Saint-Sauveur (Plihon), Delumeau (Privat), Skol Vreizh, Ouest-France Université.
Géographie de la Bretagne, Maurice Le Lannou (Plihon).
La haute-Bretagne, Jacques Levron (Arthaud).
La basse-Bretagne, Auguste Dupouy (Arthaud).
L'art breton, Henri Waquet (Arthaud).
L'art de Bretagne, V.-H. Debidour (Arthaud).
Les grandes heures littéraires de Bretagne, Charles Le Quintrec, Ouest-France.
La Bretagne de la Rance au Trégor, Bernard de Kerraoul, France-Empire.
La Bretagne et les Bretons, Maurice Le Lannou, Que sais-je ?
Les abbayes bretonnes (Fayard).
Tro-Breiz, Florian Le Roy (Librairie celtique).
Le Trégor historique et monumental, Pierre Barbier (Presses Bretonnes).
A la découverte des chapelles du Trégor, Pierre Delestre (Lescuyer Lyon).
Les Côtes-du-Nord (Richesses de France).
Châteaux de Bretagne (Hachette-Réalités).
Les enclos paroissiaux, Yannick Pelletier, Ouest-France.
Les jubés bretons, Yannick Pelletier, Ouest-France.
Les calvaires bretons, Eugène Royer, Ouest-France.
Guide Bleu, Guide Vert, A New Guide to Brittany (Ouest-France), *Guide de la Bretagne mystérieuse* (Tchou).
Ouest-France monographs.

INDEX

Cet ouvrage a été imprimé par Mame à Tours - La photocomposition est de Sécoprim à Saint-Grégoire (35) - La couverture a été imprimée par l'imprimerie Raynard à La Guerche-de-Bretagne et pelliculée par T.T.G. à Châtillon-sous-Bagneux - Maquette et mise en pages : Rozenne l'Hermitte du studio des Editions Ouest-France à Rennes - Prix à la parution en France continentale : 40 francs français.

1988 - OUEST-FRANCE - I.S.B.N. 2.7373.0146.7 - Dépôt légal : juin 1988 - N° éditeur 1467.01.05.06.88